SERMON
OUTLINES FOR

Special Days

SERMON OUTLINES FOR

Special Days

By Robert Shannon

Standard Sermon Starters
Sam E. Stone, Editor

STANDARD
PUBLISHING
Cincinnati, Ohio

The Standard Publishing Company, Cincinnati, Ohio
A division of Standex International Corporation

© 1995 by The Standard Publishing Company
All rights reserved
Printed in the United States of America

01 00 99 98 97 96 95   5 4 3 2 1

Library of Congress Cataloging-in-Publication data

Shannon, Robert, 1930-
    Sermon outlines for special days / Robert C. Shannon.
        p.   cm.
    ISBN 0-7847-0403-1
    1. Church year sermons--Outlines, syllabi, etc.
2. Occasional sermons--Outlines, syllabi, etc.   I. Title.
BV4223.S49   1995
251'.02--dc20   95-16197
                                              CIP

Table of Contents

The Church Calendar

Special Events

What a Difference a Year Makes!

Luke 2:52

Introduction

    A.   It's a common experience to see a child you've not seen for months, perhaps a distant relative or the child of a friend, and to say, "My, how you've grown!"

    B.   Will anybody be able to say of us one year from now, "My how you've grown"? We need to make a commitment to grow in the coming year as Jesus grew.

I. We Need to Grow Mentally.

    A.   We need to learn more. The one thing we will never stop being is learners (Phillipians 1:9; Colossians 1:10; 2 Peter 1:5).

    B.   We need to remember more. Jesus quoted Scripture when He was tempted. Do we know enough Scripture to get ourselves out of trouble? Do we know enough Scripture to keep from getting into trouble?

    C.   We need to understand more (Ephesians 1:8; 1 Corinthians 14:20; Colossians 1:9). It will do little good to learn and remember if we do not understand what we have learned.
        1.   Solomon urges us to apply our hearts to understanding (Proverbs 2:2).
        2.   In the Psalms we are urged to understand (Psalm 119:169).

II. We Need to Grow Physically.

    A.   All of us need to be healthier. We are God's temple.

    B.   We need to get proper rest.

    C.   We need to get proper exercise. It may be, as Paul says, that it profits little, but it does profit (1 Timothy 4:7, 8).

    D.   We need to eat a proper diet.

    E.   We need to be temperate in all things (1 Corinthians 9:25).

III. We Need To Grow Socially.

    A.   We need to be kinder to our friends (Ephesians 4:32).

Friendship is never to be taken lightly. Abraham was called "the friend of God" and Jesus called his disciples friends.

B.   We need to make friends of others (Proverbs 18:24).
Friendship can be a bridge for bringing people to Christ. Many times we try to influence people without first making them our friends. It seldom works.

C.   We need to know how to treat our enemies (Luke 6:27). Jesus not only told us how to treat our enemies, He showed us how to treat our enemies. His last miracle before the Crucifixion was for an enemy (Luke 22:50, 51). One of His last prayers was for an enemy ("Father forgive them for they know not what they do").

IV. We Need To Grow Spiritually (2 Peter 3:18).

A.   We will have to pray more.

B.   We will have to read the Bible more.

C.   We will have to give more.

D.   We will have to resist temptation more.

E.   2 Peter 1:5-7 tell us how to do this. We begin with faith. Faith alone is not enough, we must next add virtue. Faith must find its expression in character. Character demands knowledge. We must know what is right and wrong. Notice that faith is in the heart, character in the life, knowledge in the head.

Growth must be outward as well as inward. So the apostle Peter adds self-control. Children do not grow steadily, but we must grow steadily and never stop growing. This is steadfastness. Such steps will lead us to godliness and brotherly affection and love.

Conclusion

At the end of this year will God be able to say to us, "My, how you've grown"?

Illustration

Many parents make a mark on the wall by the door to indicate a child's height as the child grows year after year. If the Heavenly Father did that, would some us be shorter instead of taller, more immature instead of more mature? Or would we stand taller every year?

Love Letters Written in the Sand

John 8:3 ff.

Introduction

The title of a once popular song also fits a story in the New Testament.

I. She Didn't Understand the Difference Between Love and Lust.

A.　Many in our time do not understand the difference.

B.　We even speak of "making love" when we are really talking about lust.

C.　To miss that distinction is spiritually fatal (and often fatal to marriage as well).

II. She Didn't Know the Similarity Between Romantic Love and Spiritual Love.

A.　She didn't know that love can be given but can never be bought or sold.

B.　She may have been a prostitute. This would explain the riddle of why they didn't bring the man if they had indeed caught her in the very act. If so, she thought love could be sold.

C.　As love cannot be sold, so it cannot be bought. Gifts can express love, but they cannot buy love. Sometimes parents try to buy love. Knowing they are neglecting their children they heap extravagant gifts on them. Sometimes husbands and wives try to buy love.

D.　Love is only true love if it is given — freely given. True love is not given in response to anything. After all, Christ loved us when we were unlovely.

E.　As love must be freely given, so it must be freely received.

F.　It is unfortunate that we have only one word for love in English, but our understanding of divine love can help us understand all other loves including romantic love and family love.

G.　This means that even the love of romantic attraction should have also some element of agape love; that is of divine love.

III. She Came to Know the Difference
Between Physical Love and Spiritual Love.

A. If it is important to know the spiritual element in romantic love, it is also important to know the differences between them.

B. She may have met many men, but she had never met a man like Jesus.

C. He loved her with a spiritual love that demanded only that she sin no more. Our human love sometimes demands too much.

D. He forgave her when others condemned her.

E. Even romantic love requires forgiveness.

F. Spiritual love demands that we forgive others as we have been forgiven.

Conclusion

Sometimes it seems a handicap that we have only one word for love when the Greeks had four. But it has one advantage: we can move freely from thinking of human love to meditating on divine love.

Illustrations

Love is its own reward. Hate is its own punishment.

There is more pleasure in loving than in being loved.

Love makes us act from outward compulsion, but love makes us serve from inward compassion.

We may begin to love at first sight. We must continue to love at first slight.

There is a song titled "Love Is a Many Splendored Thing." To too many people love has become a many splintered thing.

A man said that his father had deserted their family when he himself was just a child. He said that he grew up with great resentment toward his father. Then the father became gravely ill. Every day after work the son would go by his father's apartment and care for his most basic needs. He said, "In serving him I came to love him!" While most often we will serve because we love, sometimes we will come to love because we have served.

The Example of Jesus at Communion
Luke 22:7-16

Introduction
While the universal practice of the church has been to observe the Lord's Supper on Sunday (Acts 20:7) many churches also have a special service on Thursday before Easter to commemorate the institution of the Supper. What a good time to look at the example of Jesus at Communion.

I. His Heart Was Filled With Desire.
A. He did not come out of habit, though that is a good reason to come.
   1. We ought to form good habits.
   2. Good habits seem hard to form and easy to break and bad habits seem easy to form and hard to break.
   3. It was the habit of Jesus to attend worship every week on the appointed day for Jewish worship (Luke 4:16).
   4. The apostle Paul had such a habit (Acts 17:2).
   5. Peter and John had regular habits of worship (Acts 3:1).

B. He did not come out of tradition or custom.
   1. There is value in customs and traditions.
   2. There is danger in customs and traditions (Mark 7:8).

C. He did not come out of duty.
   1. If it is good to come out of habit it is better to come out of a sense of duty.
   2. Duty seems a forgotten word in the vocabulary of modern people.
   3. We honor people who do their duty, and we should.

D. He came out of a desire.
   1. If it is good to come out of habit and better to come out of duty it is best to come out of desire.
   2. If you do not desire to be at the Lord's Table it is a symptom of a very serious spiritual disease.

II. His Heart Was Filled With Anticipation.
A. As we look backward to this event, He had looked forward to it.

B. He made preparation for it! We should prepare ourselves for this experience. Often we do not.
   1. Someone has made the obvious preparation, preparing the bread and the fruit of the vine.
   2. We have made physical preparation, washing and clothing our bodies.
   3. Have we prepared our minds and hearts?

C. We do look forward to an Upper Room — in Heaven!

III. His Heart Was Filled With Thanksgiving (1 Corinthians 11:23, 24).

A. How could He be thankful in the face of betrayal and in the face of painful death?

B. He could not give thanks for home or family. He had none. He could not give thanks for the twelve. They would soon run away. He could not give thanks for life, He was about to give His life.

C. He could be thankful for God into whose hands He would soon commit His spirit (Luke 23:46).

IV. His Heart Was Filled With Humility.

A. We see it in His willingness to sit at the same table with the betrayer.

B. We see it in His washing the disciples' feet.

V. His Heart Was Filled With Forgiveness.

A. He came ready to extend forgiveness to Judas. He symbolized this by an act of friendship recorded in John 13:26.

B. We come to receive His forgiveness.

C. We also come to extend forgiveness — to extend it to any and all who have wounded us.

The Uplifted Christ
John 12:32

Introduction

It is only a coincidence that our Lord was crucified on a hill. His death would have been just as effective if He had died in a valley. But his death on a hilltop is a very instructive coincidence — and His death by crucifixion was no coincidence at all.

I. We Feel the Pull of the Cross.

A. We are familiar with physical magnetism. We know it makes our electricity. We see it in the atom, the smallest thing we know, and in the universe, the largest thing we know. But Jesus is not talking about physical magnetism.

B. We are familiar with personal magnetism. There are those to whom people are naturally drawn. There is a force in their personalities, but that is not what Jesus is talking about.

C. We are familiar with the magnetism of influence. People are drawn to power figures: political leaders, business leaders, physicians, preachers. That is not what Jesus is talking about.

D. Jesus is talking about a spiritual magnetism that we experience every time we encounter the cross, whether in song, or sermon, picture, or thought.

E. Conversion occurs when people are drawn to Christ. It is not accomplished by driving people to Christ. It is not accomplished by luring people to Christ. It is only accomplished as they are led to Christ by their admiration of His character and love.

F. Commitment too does not occur when people are shamed into service, but when they are drawn into service by the uplifted Christ.

G. Consecrated Christian living is not induced by appeals to fear or shame. It is rather when people see the beauty of His holiness that they begin to lead pure lives.

II. We Contemplate the Puzzle of the Cross.

A. We can only partly understand the atonement.

13

B. It is such a large idea we must have a large word for it.

C. It can be understood only in the light of the Incarnation.

D. "God was in Christ" so that God Himself makes the sacrifice.
   1. The innocent makes the sacrifice for the guilty.
   2. The offended makes the sacrifice for the offender.

III. We Experience the Power of the Cross.

A. It is a powerful symbol. That is why it replaced the fish as the symbol of our faith. Today the cross is the most widely recognized symbol in the world.

B. It is a powerful lesson. In the cross we see how far sin will go. Men killed the world's one perfect person; killed the Savior of the world; killed the Son of God!

C. It is also a powerful lesson in this: it shows us how far love will go. The apostle Paul speaks of this in Romans 5: 7, 8.

D. Paul goes even further in Romans 8:32: "He who did not spare his own Son . . . how will he not also . . . graciously give us all things?"

E. It is a powerful cleanser. "What can wash away my sin? Nothing but the blood of Jesus!"

F. It is a powerful motivator. It moves us as nothing else can.

Conclusion

Can you reject such love?

Illustration

Ancient seamen believed there was a Magnetic Mountain that would pull the nails from their vessels and destroy them. There is a Magnetic Mountain — Calvary.

In Canada there is a Magnetic Hill. Your car seems to coast uphill, but it is only an illusion. Calvary is no illusion!

What's Going On Here?

Luke 24:18

Introduction

The question is amusing for Jesus was the only one who did know what was going on here.

I. Pilate Didn't Know What Was Happening.

A. To him Jesus was only another trouble-maker to be gotten out of the way.

B. He did have his doubts, though. He asked Jesus, "Are you a King."

C. He did say to those who asked for guards to stand watch over the tomb to make it as secure as they could (Matthew 27:62-65). Is there a hint of uncertainty in those words?

D. But Pilate had no idea he was sending to the cross the Savior of the world.

E. Pilate was not of royal blood. He had received his position through influence and prestige. He did not know he was condemning a King who was the Son of God.

F. Pilate didn't know that he could never destroy Jesus. That all the power of Rome could not destroy Him nor destroy the Cause He came to establish.

II. Herod Didn't Know What Was Happening.

A. He thought he was getting rid of a rival and a troublemaker. He didn't know that one can never get rid of Jesus.

B. He thought his puny guards could keep Jesus in the tomb. He didn't know it was not possible to keep Jesus in the tomb.

II. The Women Didn't Know What Was Happening.

A. If they had, they would not have wasted money buying spices for further embalming (Mark 16:1).

B. If they had, they would not have worried about rolling away the stone from the opening to the tomb (Mark 16:3).

C. If they had, they would have been neither bewildered nor afraid (Mark 16:8).

D. If they had, Mary would not have been weeping (John 20:11).

E. If they had, Mary Magdalene would not have said, "They have taken my Lord away and I don't know where they have put him" (John 20:13).

III. The Disciples Didn't Know What Was Happening.

A. To some faith was now finished. The two in our text put their faith in the past tense; "We had hoped," they said.

B. To others faith was only fiction. When the apostles heard of the resurrection the story "seemed to them like nonsense" and they did not believe (Luke 24:11).

C. To others faith was only fantasy (Mark 16:11,13; John 20:9).

D. In every resurrection appearance people are surprised to see the risen Christ (Luke 24:37).

IV. We Often Do Not Know What Happened Here.

A. We don't know that His resurrection gives assurance of the judgment (Acts 17:31).

B. We don't realize that His resurrection gives assurance of the forgiveness of sins (1 Corinthians 15:17).

C. We don't realize that His resurrection gives us our only hope (1 Corinthians 15:18,19).

Conclusion

In our text the One who knew helped those who didn't know by (1) teaching them the Scripture, (2) walking along the way in fellowship with them, and (3) by breaking bread with them.

Today we come to faith through Scripture (Romans 10:17) just as they did long ago. Our faith is confirmed in the breaking of the bread (i.e. Communion). Our faith is completed when we walk with the Lord in fellowship with Him.

Looking Forward to a Cloudy Day

Acts 1:6-11

Introduction

Some churches pay little attention to Ascension Day. Yet three of the four gospels mention the ascension of Christ. It is also described in the first chapter of Acts. And in the book of Hebrews it is prominently discussed. The Ascension is of great importance.

I. It Shows That His Work Was Finished.

A. It did not seem to be finished. There was much yet to do. There was much yet to learn.
   1. The church was not yet established.
   2. They were a comparatively small group.
   3. The message had been heard in only a small corner of the earth.

B. Still Christ said on the cross, "It is finished!"
   1. It was not a cry of resignation or defeat.
   2. It was a cry of victory.

C. If His work had been unfinished He would not have left.
   1. 1 Peter 1:18, 19
   2. Hebrews 7:27; 9:26
   3. 1 John 2:2 and 4:10

II. It Shows That Our Work Had Begun.

A. This was the occasion of our commission.

B. The timing was right.

C. The scope was universal. (Compare Matthew 28:19, 20 with Matthew 10:6, 7 and 15:24.)

D. The focus was definite.

E. The promise of Divine partnership was given.

III. It Shows That His Sacrifice Was Sufficient.

A. Hebrews 1:3; 8:1; 10:12; 12:2.

B. Jesus is now at the right hand of God the Father.

C.   No further sacrifice is needed (Hebrews 9:11-14).

D.   No further sacrifice is possible (Hebrews 10:18, 26).

IV. It Shows That Our Expectation of His Return Is Justified.

A.   The same Christ who left will return.
1.   How will we know Him?
2.   Some say we will know Him instinctively.
3.   Some say we will know Him by the nail prints in His hand.
4.   Some say we will know Him by the manner of His return. (Every eye shall see Him. There will be lightning from the east to the west.)

B.   He will return in the same way.

C.   He will not return for the same purpose.
1.   The first time He came to save (Luke 19:10).
2.   When He comes again it will be to judge (Matthew 25:31ff.).

Conclusion

The certainty of His ascension convinces us of the certainty of His return.

Illustration

Across mid-America you can see the work of the people who lived there before the American Indian. They are called the Mound Builders and you can visit the mounds they constructed. They are unusual in this: they left behind no unfinished work. Most ancient peoples left behind some unfinished temple, some unfinished palace, some unfinished city. Raphael left an unfinished painting, and Hayden an unfinished symphony, but the mound builders left behind no unfinished work. Jesus Christ was like that. He left much for His followers to do, but He finished the work He came to do.

Wind That Fills the Sails

Acts 2: 1-4; 37-41

Introduction

In coastal communities flags go up to warn people that the wind is strong and small craft should not venture out. But the church could venture out only when the wind was strong — the wind of the Spirit.

I. The Bible Predicted It.

A. Joel prophesied it (Joel 2:28).

B. John the Baptist spoke of it (Matthew 3:11).

C. John the apostle wrote about it (John 15, 16).

D. Jesus promised it (Acts 1:8; John 3:5-8).

E. This tells us that what happened at Pentecost was:
    1. No insignificant event.
    2. Long-planned by God.
    3. Important for them and for us.

II. The Apostles Experienced It.

A. The Spirit empowered them (Acts 1:8). They faced an awesome task. Without the Spirit's power they would never have attempted it. Without the Spirit's power they would never have accomplished it.

B. The Spirit filled them (Acts 2:4). They were completely led by the Spirit in a way that has not been duplicated since. There can be only one beginning. This beginning of the church was signaled by something unique and unrepeated.

C. The Spirit spoke through them (Acts 2:4) This was not only true of what they said verbally, but also of what they wrote (1 Peter 1:10, 11; 2 Peter 1:21; Hebrews 3:7; Hebrews 9:8).

D. The Spirit preserved for them the memory of Jesus and His words (John 14: 17, 26; 15:26; 16:13).

III. The Church was Strengthened by It.

A. The Spirit fired them for evangelism. The visible tongues of fire seen on one occasion were eclipsed by the burning message that they brought to a sinful and dying world.

B.   The Spirit prepared them for persecution.
  1.   The Spirit prepared Paul (Acts 20:22, 23).
  2.   The Spirit prepared others (1 Peter 1:6, 7).

C.   The Spirit comforted them in trials. Jesus even called the Holy Spirit the Comforter (John 14:15-18).

IV. The World was Amazed by It.

A.   The Spirit amazed people in the beginning (Acts 2:7). The observers at Pentecost thought the apostles were drunk.

B.   The Spirit amazes people still.
  1.   We are amazed at the survival of the church. Surely that is evidence of the presence of the Spirit in the church. The church has constantly faced strong enemies within and without, and yet endures.
  2.   We are amazed at the growth, the strength, and the progress of the church. Surely this has not been accomplished merely by the talent or genius or power of human beings.

Conclusion

The Holy Spirit empowers the church today, but only to the extent that the Spirit indwells the members and directs their lives.

Illustration

Wind is one of the many images used in the Bible to help us understand the Spirit. The force of the wind today not only drives sailboats, it makes electricity, and it has carved stone sculptures in the canyons of the American West.

If you were setting out to sea would you choose a sailboat or a rowboat? Before you decided you would ask, "Is there any wind?" If there is a wind, you choose the sailboat. Then you need not depend on your own strength.

We must ask of the church today, "Is there any wind? — any wind of the Spirit?" We must also ask the same question of our own individual lives. "Is there any wind?" Have we quenched the Spirit? Do we trust our own wisdom and power, or do we rely on Him?

The Power of Example

Ruth 1:16; 19-22

Introduction

It may seem strange on Mother's Day to choose a text about a mother-in-law, but most mothers eventually become mothers-in-law. Naomi is a good example for both.

Why did Ruth leave her own family and go to a foreign land with her mother-in-law? It seems such an unusual thing to do.

I. She Saw How Naomi Handled Herself in the Family.

A. It must have been that Ruth saw Naomi as a good mother to her sons. Otherwise Ruth would have returned to her own family .

B. It is likely that she also saw her as a good wife. Ruth herself became a good wife to Boaz. It seems likely that she took Naomi as her model.

C. It is certain that she saw Naomi as a good mother-in-law.
    1. Naomi expresses appreciation to both of her daughters-in-law (Ruth 1:8).
    2. She expresses good wishes for them. It is almost a prayer (Ruth 1:9).
    3. Their weeping shows a bond of love between them (Ruth 1:9, 14).

D. Both Naomi and Ruth were ancestors of King David and therefore ancestors of our Lord Jesus Christ.

E. It is probable that Mary's family reminded her of her distant ancestors and held up Naomi and Ruth as examples of what a good mother ought to be. Since God always chooses wisely, we can conclude that Mary, too, was a good mother.

F. This is reinforced for us when we recall how Jesus followed the commandment: "Honor thy Father and Mother."

G. This is further reinforced by the fact that when Jesus spoke about Heaven he called it home. He called it the Father's house. He must have been recalling his own home at Nazareth — a little bit of Heaven on earth. How sad it is that for many home is instead a little bit of Hell on earth!

II. She Saw How Naomi Handled Grief.

A.   The grief was real (Ruth 1:21).

B.   The grief was honest and human (Ruth 1:20).

C.   Still her grief did not destroy her faith. She complained against God (understandably) but she still believed.

III. She Saw That the Source of Naomi's Strength Lay in her Faith.

A.   We are touched by the phrase "your people will be my people" but the most important words are "and your God my God."

B.   She saw Jehovah God as superior to the gods of Moab.

C.   This was not because she had no sorrows, no tragedies, no disappointments. Faith did not isolate her from the harsh realities of life. Faith did insulate her so that they could be endured.

D.   She had this faith in spite of all that had gone wrong. This is true of many great believers in the Bible. It is certainly true of David in the Old Testament and of Paul in the New Testament. Life was not easy for them and it may not be easy for us, but faith can live in our hearts even in the most difficult circumstances.

E.   It was a tough faith — an indestructible faith.

Conclusion

We often use these words of Ruth's at weddings, but they come from a different setting and they bless and guide us today.

Illustration

Naomi gave Ruth a great gift: faith. Ruth gave Naomi a great gift: a child who was the ancestor of King David and King Jesus. Today is the day to be thankful for the things our mothers (and mothers-in-law) have given us. It is also a day to give something back to them.

There are also those surrogate mothers: people who filled the role of mother or were a mother figure to children who were not biologically theirs. Many have been blessed by foster mothers and step-mothers, and even by neighbors who provided a mother image when it was needed. Let us be thankful for them and express our thanks to them as well.

A Day to Remember
Romans 5:6-8

Introduction
What we call Memorial Day people in England call Remembrance Day. None of us intends to forget those to whom we owe so much — but it is easy to forget. It is, then, appropriate that we have a day to remember.

I. Remember Those Who Risked Their Lives for Us.
A. We have to begin with our mothers. Visit any cemetery and you will see that only a few years ago many mothers died giving birth. Today the risks of child-bearing have been greatly reduced, and such deaths are rare. Still it is true that life always begins with a woman passing under the threat of death.

B. Law enforcement officers regularly risk their lives to protect us. We often tend to think of police officers as those who inconvenience us, but many die in the line of duty and all are ready to risk their lives for us.

C. Firefighters, risk their lives to protect us and our property. They are seldom highly paid for the risks they take. They are ready night and day to come to our aid. We must not forget them.

D. We are thankful for men and women in the military who served and came home to grateful communities and to well earned retirement. They chose to risk their lives in a low-paying and sometimes difficult job.

II. Remember Those Who Lost Their Lives for Us.
A. Many died in "far-away places with strange-sounding names."

B. Some suffered pain and even torture before death came.

C. Their sacrifice was matched by parents who grieved that a son or daughter would not be coming home.

D. The widowed mates of those who paid the price for freedom and their children deserve our gratitude. They, too, paid a high price. We cannot just remember those who died. We must also remember those whose lives were shattered by their death.

E.   Freedom has always come at a high price. It would be heartless to fail to honor such sacrifice.

III. Remember One Who Gave His Life for Us All.

A.   Those who died on battlefields far away chose to serve but they did not choose to die. Their hope was always that they would survive the battle and come home.

B.   Jesus Christ came to earth knowing that he would die for us, and with the express intent of doing just that.

C.   "For this reason was I born," He said (John 18:37). For this purpose he came to earth knowing that he would die for us.

D.   We hope that those who died for country knew we'd be grateful for their sacrifice. We are certain Jesus knew that many for whom He died would be totally indifferent to His sacrifice.

E.   Those who died for country died for family and friends, not for their enemies.

F.   What is remarkable about Christ's death is that He died for us when we were enemies in our hearts and minds.

G.   Jesus' death is also unique in this: only He could have done it.

Conclusion

It is appropriate that every year we have this day to honor our countrymen who made and still make enormous sacrifices for us. It is also appropriate that every week we have a day to honor the Savior who died for the sins of the world.

Illustration

Freedom has never come cheap. That's true of political freedom, of economic freedom, and of spiritual freedom. So freedom must never be taken lightly; must never be taken for granted.

President Franklin D. Roosevelt made famous the Four Freedoms: freedom from want, freedom from fear, freedom of speech and freedom of worship. There is, of course, a fifth freedom more important than all the rest. It is freedom from sin. No government and no leader can confer that freedom. It is only given by King Jesus.

Four Little Secrets About Life
Romans 13:7

Introduction

This day is a day of honor for our graduates. We honor them with gifts and academic robes and words of congratulations. In the words of the text we honor those to whom honor is due. It is also a good time to say to them as well as to us all that we need to give honor as well as receive it. In paying honor to others we will learn four little secrets about life.

I. The Secret of Gratitude — Honor Your Father and Mother.

A. This is an important commandment (Exodus 20:12).

    1. It seems out of place among such high moral commands as "You shall not murder" and "You shall not commit adultery." There is a reason this is among the Ten Commandments.

    2. Notice the result: "that you may live long in the land."

    3. This is not a promise of personal longevity.

    4. This is a promise of national longevity. The very fabric of society and of civilization is knit together by those who honor their parents.

B. We honor by being grateful.

C. We honor by keeping the values they taught us.

D. If necessary, we honor them by taking care of their needs

II The Secret of Success — Honor Those in Authority.

A. "Fear God," wrote the apostle Peter, "honor the King" (1 Peter 2:17).

    1. The King in that time and place was wicked, but the office of King was to be honored even if the person holding the office could not be.

    2. Today we are sometimes proud of our political leaders and sometimes ashamed of our political leaders, but we honor the office whether or not we can honor the person.

    3. This means we obey the law. It means we pay our taxes. It means we are good citizens (Romans 13:1).

B. The apostle Paul said to honor our masters (1 Timothy 6:1).
 1. We have neither slaves nor masters today.
 2. The advice is still good. We have foremen, supervisors, employers, bosses. If they are in authority over us we must honor them.
 3. It means we must always do an honest day's work.
 4. It means we always do our best (Colossians 3:17).

III. The Secret of True Greatness — Honor All People.
A. Those are the exact words of the apostle Peter (1 Peter 2:17).
 1. Does this mean we honor those who do not honor us? Yes, it does.
 2. Does this mean we honor those who are very different from us? Yes, it does.
 3. Does this mean we honor those who do not even deserve honor? Yes, it does.

IV. The Secret of Salvation — Honor God.
A. Honor His name (Deuteronomy 5:11).

B. Honor His day.

C. Honor His house.

D. Honor His church.

E. Honor Him with your substance (Proverbs 3:9).

Conclusion
If we give honor in these ways we will receive even more honor than that given today. We will receive the greatest honor of all: "Well done, good and faithful servant. Come and share your master's happiness" (Matthew 25:21).

Illustrations
A little boy asked his Mother, "If the Lord gives us our daily bread, Santa brings our toys and the Stork brings babies what's the sense of having Daddy around?"

Wouldn't it be nice if everyone who is tempted to point a finger would instead hold out a helping hand?

Lessons From a Famous Father
2 Samuel 18:33

Introduction

Miles of distance and centuries of time separate us from King David. He was a king and we are commoners. Still, despite the distance and the differences we can learn much about being fathers in this present day by looking at this father of long ago.

I. Here Is a Cry of Grief.

A. Absalom was a handsome and gifted son.

B. David loved him dearly, even though David had many sons.

C. David loved him dearly, even though Absalom had committed serious sins.

D. David loved him dearly even though Absalom had tried to take the throne from his father.

E. A father's love is never conditioned on the child's conduct.

F. David's grief is not lessened by the events that preceded it, nor by Absaloms's bad character. In fact, his grief may be even greater because of it.

II. Here Is a Cry of Failure.

A. David had been immensely successful in most of the things he had done.
    1. He had been successful as a musician.
    2. He had been successful as a soldier.
    3. He had been successful as an administrator.
    4. He had been successful as a politician.

B. David failed as a father and that outweighed all his successes.
    1. In fact, David would gladly have given up his other successes if he could have traded them for success as a father.
    2. Many today give up success as a father and trade it for success in business or a profession.

C. David's failures, though, must be seen in true perspective.
    1. Fathers must accept some responsibility for the character of

their children. They have a responsibility to set a good example, and to teach moral values.

2. Fathers must not accept full responsibility for the character of their children. There are other influences that enter every life. Also, it must be remembered that every person is a free moral agent. Some fathers are carrying a load of guilt they do not need to carry.

III. It Is a Cry of Futility.

A. David could not die for his son.
   1. A father can die for his child in the sense that he can die to protect the child. Most fathers would willingly do that.
   2. A father cannot die for his child in the sense that the father's dying will keep the child from ever facing death. All of us must die.

B. The Lord Jesus Christ could and did die for us.
   1. Romans 5:6; 5:18; 1 Corinthians 15:3; 22; Romans 6:8.
   2. We still have to suffer physical death, but it has lost its sting (1 Corinthians 15:54-56).
   3. We do not have to suffer the death that is the wages of sin (Romans 6:23; 8:1).

Conclusion

While we learn much that is helpful from the example of David, we learn the most from the example of God. It is very important to remember that in the Bible God is described as a Father. God represents fatherhood at its very best.

Illustration

Six year old Tommy came downstairs crying. "What's the matter?" asked his Mother.

"Daddy just hit his thumb with a hammer, " the boy replied.

"A big boy like you shouldn't cry over a thing like that," said the Mother. "Why didn't you laugh?"

"I did," he replied.

The Worth of a Child

Psalm 127:3

Introduction

While we make much of Mother's Day in every church and sometimes pay attention to Father's Day we often overlook the more important special event on the calendar, Children's Day.

I. The Value of Children Was not Generally Celebrated in Bible Times.

A. This was true in Old Testament times. That's why this text was necessary.

B. This was true in New Testament times. That's why people were so surprised that Jesus had time for children (Matthew 19:14).

II. Parents and Grandparents Recognize the Value of Children.

A. Godly parents see the need to set an example for their children.

B. Thoughtful parents recognize that children set an example for us.
   1. They set us an example of innocence.
   2. They set us an example of forgiveness.
   3. They set us an example of love.
   4. They set us an example of joy.

C. The value grandparents place on children is legendary. "Let me tell you about my grandchildren" is a common statement.

D. We see the spiritual possibilities of this in the New Testament in 2 Timothy 1:5.

E. We see the spiritual possibilities of this in the Old Testament in the life of Josiah, who did not walk in the evil ways of his father Amon but in the righteous ways of his great grandfather Hezekiah.

III. Childless Couples Recognize the Value of Children.

A. One out of five couples cannot have children.

B. They endure great indignities trying to solve the problem of infertility.

C. They go to great expense to adopt children.

D. We should recognize the grief of infertile couples and give them our support and comfort.

E. We should remember that it is not necessarily a virtue to bear a child and it is certainly not a punishment to be childless.

F. We should note that many who are not parents have a parental heart.

IV. Surrogate Parents Recognize the Value of Children.

A. Many times a childless person becomes a mother image or a father image to someone else's child. Sometimes it is the child of a relative, sometimes the child of a neighbor, sometimes a child in the church.

B. Great blessings have come to children because of these people.

V. The Church Must Recognize the Value of Children.

1. Ephesians 6:1,4.
2. Colossians 3:20,21.
3. 1 Timothy 3:4, 12.
4. Titus 2:1-5.

Conclusion

The church is the body of Christ. Surely the spiritual body of Christ should say today, what Christ said when He was in his physical body: "Let the little children come to me" (Mark 10:14).

Illustration

The Romanian word for children is *copii,* which when it is pronounced sounds a lot like the English word copy. No parent would like a child to be a carbon copy of the parent, but often that is what they become. That fact should make us all take far more seriously the kind of examples we set for those who will come after us. Even children who do not want to be like their parents, often end up acting much like them.

The Nation Whose God Is the Lord
Psalm 33:12

Introduction
While this verse may have originally applied to the nation of Israel, it is obvious that the principle here applies to any nation or to all nations.

I. A Godless Nation.
A. Many say that our nation is godless. There is certainly much to suggest that this saying is true.
  1. There is such a lowering of moral standards that many do not at all take seriously the Ten Commandments.
  2. There is a disregard for personal property.
  3. There is a disregard for personal purity.
  4. There is even a disregard for human life.
  5. There is a disregard for laws, whether man's or God's.

B. The thought of a godless nation is chilling.
  1. It is like shepherdless sheep.
  2. It is like a fatherless child.

II. The Nation That Is not Godless at All.
A. One might say that our nation is not godless. The problem is that the nation has too many gods.
  1. There is the god of success.
  2. There is the god of money.
  3. There is the god of pleasure.
  4. There is the god of sex.
  5. There is the god of fame.
  6. There is the god of power.

B. With so many gods, is it surprising that the one true God is forgotten?

III. The Nation Whose God Is the Lord.
A. When the text was written there were many gods. Most nations had several. Some had hundreds.

B. Jehovah declares again and again that He is a zealous God and will permit no rivals. This idea of monotheism changed the world.

C. What is necessary for a nation to be able to say that their God is the Lord?
    1. They must honor His laws.
    2. They must respect His name.
    3. They must honor His day.
    4. They must respect His house.
    5. Above all, they must respect Him!

D. What is the result when a nation honors God?
    1. They have less turmoil and unrest within.
    2. They have more compassion for helping those who are without.
    3. They have a heightened sense of security.
    4. Perhaps we have yet to see how many blessings might come to any nation that takes this text seriously.

Conclusion

On a day when one looks back to the founding of this nation; on a day when we are grateful for the wisdom and the sacrifices of the past; it is good to look ahead to what can be in the future.

Illustrations

The makers of caps have gone beyond advertising to putting some humorous and whimsical mottoes on their products. One cap said, "I am Their Leader. Which Way Did They Go?"

Someone has humorously suggested that if native Americans had had a more strict immigration policy our country wouldn't be in the mess it is now! Since most of us are descended from immigrants, we can be thankful that our ancestors did get to come to this land. We should not be surprised that other people want to come and share our freedoms, nor should we be selfish in sharing them.

To the Work! To the Work!

Proverbs 6: 6-11

Introduction

In the Caribbean islands, as in most tropical lands, people move more slowly. They don't get in a hurry as we who live in the temperate climate sometimes do. A missionary in Jamaica was noted for her high level of energy. A man in the church spoke of it to a visiting American. He said, "Mrs. Herget acts as if work were a virtue." It is!

I. The Bible Teaches Us About Work.

    A.   It is taught in the Old Testament.

        1.   There are more than twelve verses in the book of Proverbs alone that teach that work is a virtue.

        2.   When we read the fourth commandment in Exodus 20 we miss part of it. Not only does the text say "Remember the Sabbath day." It also says, "Six days you shall labor."

        3.   The writer of Ecclesiastes says, "Whatever your hand finds to do, do it with all your might" (Ecclesiastes 9:10).

    B.   It is taught in the New Testament.

        1.   Jesus said He came to serve, not to be served.

        2.   He said, "The workers are few."

        3.   In a famous parable He told of an employer asking the important question: "Why have you been standing here all day long doing nothing?" (Matthew 20:6).

        4.   The apostle Paul said that he himself worked hard (1 Corinthians 4:12).

        5.   He said we should work hard (Colossians 3:23).

        6.   He taught others to work (1 Thessalonians 4:11).

        7.   He said we should respect those who work (1 Thessalonians 5:12).

        8.   He said those who would not work should not eat (2 Thessalonians 3:10).

II. The Bible Gives Us Examples of Workers.

    A.   The apostle Paul gave himself as an example for the leaders at Ephesus (Acts 20:34,35).

B. Jesus gave us an example in work.
   1. He worked in the carpenter shop at Nazareth.
   2. He worked as a teacher and healer. No one ever crowded more activity into three and one-half years than Jesus did during his ministry.
   3. He said, "I work."
C. God himself is an example of work.
   1. Jesus said, "My Father works, and I work."
   2. God is introduced to us as a worker. How does Genesis begin? Not with some statement about the nature of God but with His work. "In the beginning God created!"
   3. When He chose people to serve, God chose busy people.
      a. Gideon was threshing wheat.
      b. Moses was tending sheep.
      b. Saul was working on his father's farm.
      c. David was tending sheep.
      d. Amos was gathering fruit.
      e. Peter, Andrew, James and John were fishing.
      f. Matthew was collecting taxes.
      g. The only exception is Nathaniel who was sitting under a shade tree, and I like to think that he had been working and had just stopped to rest.

Conclusion

If work is a virtue then laziness is a sin (Hebrews 6:12).

Illustration

A retired missionary had come back to the United States to spend his declining years on the campus of a Christian college. He was disturbed by what he regarded as the poor work habits of the students. When he preached in the college chapel he spoke of it. "If you aren't careful." he said, "some of you will die in bed. And it would serve you right!" To him there could be no greater disgrace.

Danger Ahead

Colossians 3:5

Introduction

We are often warned of danger. We see a sign: "Beware of Dog" and we enter the property with caution. We read on a bottle: "Danger! Poison!" and we are careful where we store it. We see a sign: "Danger! High Voltage Electricity" and keep our distance. We see another sign: "Warning! Railroad Crossing" and we stop, look and listen.

When the apostle Paul wrote to the Colossians he gave them a warning that they needed. It may be that we, too, need to heed the warning of this text.

I. Here Is a Danger to be Avoided.

A. It is a danger as great as the temptation to sexual sin.

B. We are shocked to see covetousness on the same list with fornication.

C. When we say a person is immoral we almost always mean sexually immoral. We never mean that that person is not generous.

D. Jesus also warned us. He said, "Be on your guard against all kinds of greed" (Luke 12:15).

E. Jesus did not say this because He wanted to defraud us of something. Paul did not write this because He wanted to get something from us. Both saw this as a serious danger.

F. Why is greed such a serious sin?
1. Because it tempts us not to trust God.
2. Because it tempts us to trust in ourselves (Psalm 118: 8,9).
3. Because it denies that everything already belongs to God (Psalm 24:1).
4. Because the love of money is the root of all kinds of evils (1 Timothy 6:10).
5. Because the temptation is so subtle.

II. Here Is a Definition to be Believed.

A. We are further surprised to find Paul saying that covetousness is idolatry.

35

B.   We think of idolatry as something that belongs to a long dead
     past when men carved idols of stone or cast images of gold or
     silver.

C.   We think that idolatry, if it exists at all today, exists in some far
     off place where primitive people worship trees or stones.

D.   The fact is that idolatry is a very present danger to us today.
     1.   This is so in spite of the fact that we stamped on our coins:
          "In God We Trust."
     2.   This is so because the worship of anything other than God is
          idolatry.
     3.   Sometimes we worship power and money will buy us
          power.
     4.   Sometimes we worship fame, and money will buy us fame.
     5.   Sometimes we worship success and for many money is the
          measure of success.
     6.   Sometimes we worship security and we think (wrongly) that
          money will buy us security. However money will not take
          care of us. We have to take care of money!
     7.   Whenever or wherever we put our trust in anyone or any-
          thing other than God we have become guilty of idolatry.

Conclusion

We need to avoid this sin as carefully as we avoid sexual sin. We need
to protect ourselves from this temptation just as we do from other
temptations. We need to give to keep ourselves from sin!

Illustration

A little girl gave her father a present for Father's Day. She picked it out
herself and bought it. Where did she get the money? From her father,
of course, but the love was hers. When you give something to God it
is just like that. He gives you the means to do it, but the love is yours.

We give Thee but Thine own
What e'er the gift may be.
All that we have is Thine alone
A trust, O Lord, from Thee.
— William W. How

Higher Ground

Psalm 100

(Note: This sermon uses the inductive pattern. In preaching sermons of this type the text is sometimes introduced at the end rather than at the beginning.)

Introduction

There are several levels of gratitude, each one higher than the one before. Today is a day to remember an old song and pray: "Lord, plant my feet on higher ground!"

I. Expressing Thanks Is Habit.

A. It's a good habit. We do it automatically.

B. We need to form good habits and keep them.

C. It is no sin to be in the habit of thanking people for the things they do for us.

D. It is no sin to be in the habit of thanking God at every meal.

E. Thanksgiving is habit, but it is more than habit.

II. Expressing Thanks Is Courtesy.

A. We expect it of others and they expect it of us.

B. That is a valid expectation. It is etiquette. It is good manners.

C. God expects us to be thankful. Surely He has a right to expect us to extend to Him the same courtesy we commonly extend to people.

D. To fail to thank God would be rude and thoughtless.

E. Thanksgiving is courtesy, but it is more than courtesy.

III. Expressing Thanks Is Worship.

A. It is a part of pagan worship. We can find many examples in which heathen people thank their gods.

B. It was an integral part of Old Testament worship. The Old Testament is filled with examples of personal thanksgiving and of corporate thanksgiving.

37

C. The New Testament is also filled with examples. We can find them in the life of Jesus, in the life of the apostle Paul, and in the life of the church.

D. Our own contemporary worship experiences highlight thanksgiving. It is in our songs, in our public prayers, in our sermons and in our meditations.

E. Thanksgiving is worship, but it is more than worship

IV. Expressing Thanks Is Faith.

A. It is believing that past blessings came from God.

B. It is believing that present blessings come from God.

C. It is believing that future blessings will come from God.

D. Thanksgiving is faith, but it is more than faith.

V. Expressing Thanks Is Love.

A. Love means we never take our gifts for granted.

B. Love means we never take the Giver for granted.

C. Love should be expressed in words.

D. Love should be expressed in deeds.

Conclusion

It is better to thank God from habit than not to thank Him at all; better to thank Him from courtesy than not to thank Him at all. It is good to thank God in worship, better to thank Him from faith, best of all to thank Him from love.

Illustration

We have all seen a parent nudging a child and saying, "What do you say?" and the child parrots, "Thank you." It's a good way to teach a child — but we should never have to nudge believers and say, "What do you say to the nice God?" No, thanksgiving should come from hearts so filled with gratitude we cannot keep still.

And Now, for an Important Announcement
Luke 2:8-17

Introduction

Most church-goers dread announcements. Announcements are considered dull, but not this announcement.

I. It Was Personal — "to you."

A. The shepherds were surprised at what they saw and heard. They did not expect to hear such songs or see such sights.

B. We are surprised that shepherds were chosen to receive this greatest of all announcements. We would expect that the heavenly choir would sing for a prestigious audience. Can you imagine the Metropolitan Opera putting on a performance for illiterate herdsmen?

C. We may never know why they were chosen, but the fact that they were chosen is a comfort to all of us ordinary people.

D. Paul suggests a possible reason in 1 Corinthians 1:26-29. God often chooses humble things for grand purposes, and ordinary people to do extraordinary deeds.

E. Now centuries later we must sill hear the message as a personal message. The fact that hundreds of years have passed and thousands upon thousands have heard must not diminish the impact of the message. It is still personal!

II. It Was Universal — "for all people."

A. The fact that it was universal does not contradict the fact that it was personal.

B. It was personal in impact, but universal in scope. All people were to have the opportunity to respond individually and personally to a God who loves them individually and personally.

C. The fact that the announcement is universal destroys any ethnic pride that we may have.

D. This fact also makes us humble. God's chosen people today are those who choose to believe.

E. It makes us evangelistic. God wants us to share the message with everyone.

F. It gives us missionary zeal. God wants us to share the message in every place.

G. The apostle Peter learned that God is no respecter of persons. (Acts 10:34,35) His words "every nation" were the proper response to Jesus' words "all nations."

III. It Was Timely — "today."

A. Spiritually it seems that every Christmas we are celebrating the birth of Christ for the first time.

B. Nationally and internationally we seem to need Christmas especially at this time.

C. Perhaps in your life Christmas has special meaning this year.

D. We must never be content with simply recalling a past event.

E. The famous Christmas carol says "Be born in us today!"

IV. It Was Also Timeless — "a Savior."

A. That's what people needed then.

B. That's what people need now.

C. That's what people have needed in all the years between then and now.

D. That's what people will need until the end of time.

Conclusion

It is never enough to just listen to the announcement even if we listen attentively. It is not enough to just listen to the announcement, even if we listen reverently. We must respond to this angelic announcement.

Illustration

While it is proper to pay special attention to these verses in December, it is equally true that they are important to us every day of the year. On any Sunday we could appropriately sing, "Joy to the World, the Lord is Come!" At any time of the year we could appropriately sing "O Come All Ye Faithful."

Long Shadows

Acts 5:12-15

Introduction

On the anniversary of the founding of this church, it is fitting that we should look back and celebrate the past. It is also fitting that we should look ahead and be challenged by the future.

I. The Apostle Casts a Long Shadow.

A. His Shadow fell on them.

    1. It was not a shadow to fear. Acts 5:13 does not mean that people were afraid of the apostles. It only means that they held both the apostles and the church in awe and reverence. Today we need this same respect for the church.

    2. It was a healing shadow. The apostle Peter never performed a miracle to hurt, only to heal.

    3. It was a helping shadow. Many who came were people who had no other help. Without the miracle of apostolic healing they would never have gotten well.

    4. The shadow of Peter's influence was longer than his physical shadow.

B. His shadow falls on us.

    1. All believers have been blessed by the shadow of this apostle.

    2. We are instructed by his sermons. One man called Peter's sermon in Acts 2 the greatest sermon ever preached. He was well aware of the preaching of Jesus, but noted that Jesus' preaching was necessarily incomplete because Jesus had not yet died. Peter's great sermon on Pentecost was the first after the cross and resurrection. We are all instructed by it.

       a. We learn the subject of all great preaching — Jesus. The sermon began with Jesus of Nazareth and ended with Jesus as Lord and Christ (Acts 2:22; 2:36).

       b. We learn the object of all great preaching — that people might be saved (Acts 2:40).

       c. We learn what we need to do (Acts 2:38).

       d. We learn what Christ will do for us (Acts 2:38).

    3. We are comforted by Peter's failures. Though he often spoke when he should have been listening, Christ could use him.

Though he denied the Lord, he was forgiven and given another chance.

4. We are strengthened by his courage. It was he who brought the sword, and used it, in Gethsemane.

II. This Church Casts a Very Long Shadow.

A. The shadow of this church is longer than the shadow cast by the building in which the church meets.

B. This church casts its shadow all over the community; wherever its members live lives of blessed influence.

C. This church casts its shadow over other churches. They are encouraged by the example set here.

D. The church's shadow reaches across the country through our ministry of benevolence and home missions.

E. The church's shadow reaches beyond this country through foreign missions.

F. Always it must be a healing shadow. It must never be a hurtful shadow.

Conclusion

As long as the shadow of this church is, it must be longer still.

Illustration

Your personal physical shadow changes. Sometimes it is very short, sometimes it is very long. The difference is determined by your relationship to the sun. So the church's shadow is determined by its relationship to the Son, S-o-n.

We tend to think of shadows as unpleasant things; things to be feared. But if you lived in the desert you would think of shadows as lovely things. To the traveler the shadow is a shade where he may rest. In the shadows plants grow even in the desert. In the shadow of a rock moisture condenses to sustain life in the desert. And when one is lost, with no visible landmarks, shadows point the way.

Help! We're Parents!

Judges 13:8

Introduction

Many churches hold a special service of dedication when a baby is born to someone in the church family. Of course, in the larger sense, parents cannot dedicate the baby. They can only dedicate themselves. In the largest sense the church dedicates itself to help, to nurture, to support and to guide.

We turn today to one of the Bible's oldest books. Sometimes we think that ancient people have nothing to teach us. They rode on camels. We live in the jet age. But all the problems and opportunities that we face they faced. In this text Manoah and his wife experienced both the pain of infertility and the joy of approaching parenthood. We can learn from them.

I. They *Felt* Inadequate for the Task.

A. They were inadequate for the task.
   1. They had long been childless (Judges 13:2).
   2. They had no experience in parenting.
   3. They knew that they must raise their child in a difficult environment. Paganism was strong in the land. Immorality was rampant.
   4. They knew they must provide a counterweight to these influences.

B. Every parent feels inadequate for the task.
   1. We, too, must raise our children in a difficult environment.
   2. We, too, must have an influence that will outweigh the influence of the world around us.

II. They *Were* Inadequate for the Task.

A. Parenting is never easy, especially for first-time parents.

B. Even those with experience in parenting are sometimes baffled by its complexities.

C. We live in a world that is often hostile to our values.

D. We know that there are influences and forces that are beyond our control.

E.   The only experts on child-rearing are those who never had any.

III. The Lord *Is* Adequate.

A.   Manoah did right to pray for guidance. So do we.

B.   His was to be a special child (Judges 13:3-7).

C.   But in some sense every child is a special child.

D.   Manoah did right to seek counsel from the man of God.

E.   We will do well to seek the best advice we can get.

Conclusion

The conclusion to this story is a sad one (Judges 14:1-3). Manoah and his wife could not bring themselves to deny the young man something he wanted — a mistake many parents make. Still, all parents must know that every child, like Samson, has a free will. We do our best, but the choice is eventually the child's.

Illustrations

Someone has said that a baby is God's opinion that the world should go on.

A certain father had a little daughter who kept a daily notebook. On one page she drew a picture of her father and carefully printed his name and address. When asked why, she explained. She had been watching a movie about amnesia. She said, "If I ever forget who I am I want everybody to know who I belong to."

Samson forgot to whom he belonged. Every child must come to know that he or she does not just belong to Mother and Dad. The child also belongs to the church — the community of faith. And most importantly, the child belongs to God.

When they tempted Jesus with the coin for taxes he asked, "Whose image is this?" They answered, "Caesars's." Jesus replied, "Render therefore to Caesar the things that are Caesar's and to God the things that are God's" If I put a child in the midst and ask "Whose image is this?" some would say the image of his father, or the image of her mother. More than that, every child bears the image of God. Give to Ceasar what is Ceasar's, and to God what is God's.

Beginning Again

Titus 3:3-8

Introduction

We often refer to John 3:5 where Jesus spoke of being born again. We need to pair it with Titus 3:5 where Paul gives the details of newness in Christ.

I. Here Is One Marvelous Change.

A. The apostle Paul uses four words to describe this one wonderful change (saved, washing, regeneration, renewal) but all describe a single event.

B. It is marvelous because of the condition from which we have been saved.
   1. Foolish.
   2. Disobedient.
   3. Slaves.
   4. Living in pleasure.
   5. Living in malice and envy.
   6. Hated and hating.

C. It is marvelous because of the condition to which we have been brought.
   1. Justified.
   2. Heirs of eternal life.

II. Here Are Two Important Facts.

A. We are not saved by works of righteousness.

B. We are saved by God's mercy and grace.

III. Here Are Three Significant Symbols.

A. We are washed.
   1. There is a washing that is symbolic. Baptism involves the use of water, the universal agent of cleansing.
   2. There is a washing that is more than symbolic.
      a. The apostle Paul said so (Ephesians 5:26; 1 Corinthians 6:11).

        b.   The preacher Ananias said so (Acts 22:16).

        c.   The apostle James said so (James 4:8).

        d.   The apostle John said so (1 John 1:7).

        e.   The apostle Peter said so (Acts 2:38).

        f.   The writer of Hebrews said so (Hebrews 9:14).

        g.   The Lord Jesus said so (John 15:3).

B.   We are born again. The word regeneration in Titus 3:5 means the same thing as the words born again in John 3:5.

C.   We are renewed.
    1.   The apostle Paul loved this term.
        a.   He wrote of a new life (Romans 6:4).
        b.   He wrote of a new mind (Romans 12:2).
        c.   He wrote of a new attitude (Ephesians 4:23).
        d.   He wrote of a new self (Ephesians 4:24).
        e.   He wrote of a new creature (2 Corinthians 5:16).
    2.   The apostle Peter loved this term (1 Peter 1:3).

IV. Here Are Four Attributes of God.

A.   His goodness.

B.   His loving kindness.

C.   His mercy.

D.   His grace.

Conclusion

What we do today is only in response to what God has already done. It is always true that we are saved by grace. It is always true that we are washed in the blood, even though we are baptized in water. What we do today is highly significant. It shows our willingness to obey Christ's commands. It shows our understanding of the proper response to grace. It illustrates the benefits of salvation. Most of all it illustrates the great deeds of Christ' death, burial and resurrection.

Let Us Break Bread Together
2 Kings 4:42-44

Introduction

We learn by comparison. What is it like? We teach by comparison. It is like this. So this text in 2 Kings brings to mind some things we know about the Lord's Supper. Of course, the text teaches us nothing about the Supper. It only illustrates what is taught in other texts. But the illustrations are useful, the comparisons helpful.

I. The Bread Comes to Us as a Gift.

A. In the text a man gave twenty loaves to the man of God and he in turn gave to one hundred men.

B. The most important gift is Christ himself, for whom the Supper stands. 2 Corinthians 9:15 calls Him the "indescribable gift."

C. But the Supper is also God's gift, given to us by Christ on His way to the cross.

D. Have you ever received, not a gift, but only a picture of it? The gift had been ordered, but had not yet arrived. The picture was a symbol of that gift. It represented the gift as this bread represents Christ.

II. The Bread Is a Gift of Firstfruits.

A. The bread was made from the first ripe grain: the first of the harvest.

B. Paul says in 1 Corinthians 15:23 that Christ is the firstfruits of the resurrection.

C. If you grew up on a farm in the temperate zone you can remember a taste of those first spring vegetables from the garden and those first spring fruits from the orchard.

D. In every land there is a festival of the harvest. The Jews called theirs Pentecost. It was on that day that the promised Holy Spirit came upon the apostles and the church was born.

E. Since God thinks of us first, not last, should we not think of Him first, not last ?

III. The Bread Is Always Sufficient.

A. The man who gave the bread was afraid there would not be enough and he would be embarrassed. The prophet Elisha assured him that there would be enough for everyone.

B. Bread and water is a poor diet, physically. But Jesus as the Bread of Life and the Water of Life is all we need.

C. There is always enough time. Some think we rush through the Supper without enough time for contemplation. But that great Passover meal, which also illustrates Communion was eaten in haste.

D. Perhaps our Lord measures the service not by its length, but by its breadth and depth. How deeply do we meditate? That is more important than how long we commune.

IV. There Is Always Something Leftover.

A. Christians are not agreed as to what should be done with the left-over bread and wine, but there is a more important concern. There are other things left over.

B. The taste is on our tongues but a moment, the food in our stomachs only a few hours, but the memory of what happened at the table should stay with us for a whole week.

C. The Presence we encountered at the table should also stay with us all the week through.

Conclusion

Even when we have considered all these parallels we know that the Lord's Supper is unique. It may in many respects be like other meals, but in some respects it is like no other meal ever eaten. That is why we come to it with such deep reverence.

Illustrations

A man said that one Christmas the only thing he gave his son was a piece of paper, a very small piece of paper. It was a gift certificate. He could take that piece of paper to the store and get anything he wanted. One of the ways Christ comes to us is through Communion. It is our gift certificate.

The Joy of Paying Taxes

Matthew 22:15-22

Introduction

You would naturally expect a preacher to say something religious, even to an audience like this, and I will. You would also expect a preacher to select some popular subject for an occasion like this, and I have. I want to talk about taxes. Isn't that a fun subject? What could make a person more popular than to speak about taxes!

The fact is, that Jesus said something about taxes — and it's most helpful.

I. We Have a Duty to Government.

A.   We have this duty even if it is not a government of our own choosing. I don't know how you voted last time and I'm not going to tell you how I voted last time, but in the days of Jesus nobody voted any time.

B.   Theirs was a wicked government, yet they had a duty to it. The apostle Paul agreed with this (Romans 13:1).

C.   What is our duty to government? What should we give to Caesar?
   1.   It is our duty to pay taxes. We don't have to enjoy paying them but we have to pay them. We have to pay them even if the government is wasting the money. That gives us no right to evade our taxes.
   2.   It is our duty to obey the law. This is true even if the law seems unjust, unfair or just plain stupid. We are free to work to change laws, but we are not free to disobey laws, unless they conflict with God's law.
   3.   It is our duty to respect the office of leaders whether or not we happen to respect the person who holds the office at any given time. When the apostle Peter said, "Honor the King" the King was a person not worthy of honor. but the office of King was to honored (1 Peter 2:17).
   4.   It is our duty to try to make government better.

II. We Have a Duty to God.

A.   If we give to Caesar the things that are Caesar's we must also give to God the things that are God's. What are the things that are God's?

1. Time belongs to God. We ought to spend it wisely and spend some of it in the service of the community and the service of our fellow man.
2. Our abilities belong to God. If you have a talent, use it. Don't waste it. And use it to be a blessing to somebody.
3. Our energies belong to God. We ought not waste our energies on trivial things, but on things that matter.
4. Our hearts belong to God. We must always care.
   a. We must care about the less fortunate.
   b. We must care about the disadvantaged and the handicapped.
   c. We must care about the poor.
   d. We must care about children.
   e. We must care about our schools.
   f. We must care about our community.

B. When we render the proper things to both Caesar and God we discover the two sides to this text work together. Loyalty to government and loyalty to God strengthen each other.

Conclusion

Jesus lived a long time ago in a far away land under a system far different from our own, but what He said then can guide and bless us here and now.

Illustration

In northern Scotland are two outstanding mountains called Ben Hope and Ben Loyal. In the Gaelic language ben means "a mountain peak." One wonders why they are named Hope and Loyal. Certainly hope towers above all the other intangibles of life. We can live without love. We can live without faith. We can live without friends. We can even live without health. We can live without money. We cannot live without hope. Loyalty towers above all other human virtues. The disloyal we call traitors. Many children have been named for George Washington; none for Benedict Arnold.

Dedicating an Unfinished Building
Matthew 16:13-18

Introduction

It is proper that we should build buildings such as this. It is proper that they should not only be functional, but beautiful They are a testimony to all who pass by. It is proper that we should celebrate the completion of such a building with a ceremony of thanksgiving for the gifts and sacrifices that made it possible, and with a time of dedication of both the building and ourselves.

I. Jesus Chose to Compare a Church to a Building.

A. Each must have an architect.
1. The designer of the universe designed the church (John 1:3).
2. He is the world's only truly creative designer.

B. Each must have a strong foundation. No building lasts longer than its foundation (1 Corinthians 3:11; Hebrews 13:8).

C. Each must incorporate a variety of materials.
1. Wood and steel and glass and stone are brought together in harmonious union in this material building.
2. The same is true of the spiritual building (1 Corinthians 3:12; 12:12-26).

II. Jesus Chose the Place to Make This Comparison.

A. It was not at Bethlehem where He was born. It was not at Nazareth where He grew up. It was not at Capernaum where He had his headquarters. It was not at Jerusalem the capital of the nation.

B. It was at Caesarea Phillipi.
1. That place was on the high ground, literally.
2. That place was the headwaters of the Jordan river, and these words were the fountainhead of His ministry.
3. That had been a place of pagan worship. Here they worshipped Him.
4. That place was named for two kings: Caesar and Herod Phillip. Here stood the King of Kings.

III. He Chose the Audience Carefully.

A. This announcement was not made to the multitudes.

B. It was made to the select few whom He had chosen.

IV. He Chose the Time Carefully.

A. It was not at the beginning of His ministry; nor when He was baptized, nor when He began to preach and heal.

B. It was not at the end of His ministry after the glory of the resurrection.

C. It was not on the cross.

D. It was at the mid-point in His ministry.

V. He Chose His Words Carefully.

A. He compared the church to a building.

B. He said it would be future to that moment in time.

C. He said that He would build it. Oddly enough, though, the church did not begin until after He had left earth. He built it, but He did it through His disciples. Today, He still works through His followers.

D. He said that it would belong to Him..

E. He said that it would endure. This building may last for fifty years, or a hundred, but it will not last forever. The church will endure throughout eternity.

Conclusion

It is because we understand the true and invisible church that we have built this visible expression of our faith.

Illustration

On the island of Maui, one of the Hawaiian islands, there is a church called the Miracle Church. It was built of coral. Before construction began a storm swept a huge pile of coral onto the shore. They used it to build the church. When they were finished another storm came and carried the leftover coral back into the sea. That will not happen for us — either materially or spiritually. We shall have to build up the church ourselves.

Two Certainties

Psalm 103:13, 14

Introduction

Life holds many mysteries. Death is a mystery, too. There is so much today that we don't understand. I would be less than honest with you if I told you that I understand the events that bring us to this place. I do not come to you with explanations. I do come to you with two blessed certainties from this ancient text. I am as certain of these two facts as I am certain that I am standing here before you.

I. We Can Be Certain About God's Knowledge.

A. He knows us because He made us. He remembers that we are dust.

B. He knows us because He knows all things.

C. That which is hard for us to understand is plain to Him.

D. Job asked, "Can anyone teach knowledge to God?" (Job 21:22).

E. In Isaiah 40:13,14 the prophet speaks of the knowledge of God.

F. God has not promised to tell us everything He knows. He has the answers to our questions; the solutions to our riddles. He may reveal them to us in time, or He may not.

G. Paul said that now we know in part, but will someday know more fully (1 Corinthians 13:12).

H. An old song says, "We'll understand it better by and by." Many questions will be answered in time — or in eternity. It may be that we will not understand everything but we will understand many things better "by and by."

II. We Can Be Certain About God's Love.

A. In our text God is described as being like a Father. That doesn't mean that God is like your father or my father. It does mean that God embodies fatherhood at its best. He is the ideal Father.

B. God revealed Himself to Moses as merciful and gracious, long-suffering, abounding in goodness and truth, forgiving iniquity and transgression and sin (Exodus 34:6).

C. David saw God as a refuge and wrote "in the day of trouble . . . He will hide me" (Psalm 27:5). He said, "God is our refuge and strength, an ever present help in trouble" (Psalm 46:1).

D. So we know that God cares about us always.

E. If He cares about us always He certainly cares about us today.

Just when I need Him Jesus is near.
Just when I falter, Just when I fear.
Ready to comfort, Ready to cheer,
Just when I need Him most.
— Wm. Poole

F. It was said of Jesus that he would bear our griefs and carry our sorrows (Isaiah 53:4).

G. Somehow our grief is easier to bear when we know we do not bear it alone.

H. That is why the presence of friend and family is so precious to us today.

I. It means even more to know that God is not far removed from the scene of our sorrow, but is here present today.

Conclusion

We believe in God's love even when it does not seem that He loves us. The facts may seem to suggest otherwise, but our faith insists that God loves us as a father loves his children, pities us as a father pities his children, forgives us as a father forgives his children, and comforts us as a father comforts his children.

When God Looks for a Partner

Judges 7:18

(Background Scripture Judges Chapters 6,7,8)

Introduction

God was looking for a partner. It was not because God could not defeat the Midianites alone. It was because God chose to work through human instrumentality. This is often the case in both Old Testament and New. When God looks for a partner, what kind of person does He want?

I. When God Looks for a Partner He Looks for a Person of Faith.

A. Gideon's faith did not come easily. Perhaps our faith will not always come easily.

B. Gideon's faith increased after the miracle of the fleece.

C. Gideon showed his faith by naming the altar he built, "Jehovah Shalom" (The Lord is Peace). He did this before the battle had even been fought — before the victory had been won.

II. When God Looks for a Partner He Looks for an Obedient Person.

A. God said, "Tear down the pagan altar" and Gideon tore it down.

B. God said, "Build an altar to me." Gideon did it.

C. God said, "Reduce your army!" and Gideon did.

D. God instructed Gideon to arm them with pitchers and trumpets and lamps and Gideon did.

III. When God Looks for a Partner He Looks for a Humble Person.

A. Judges 6:15

B. When the angel said, "The Lord is with you, mighty warrior," Gideon must have looked behind him to see what person the angel was addressing.

C. He did not think of himself as a mighty warrior or a man of courage. Mighty men of courage do not thresh their wheat by the winepress to hide it from the Midianites.

D. When God finished with him he was a man of courage. He went through the whole country sounding a trumpet.

IV. When God Looks for a Partner He Looks for a Person who Seeks No Praise.

A. A great victory was won, but some could only criticize (Judges 8:1).

B. Have you ever had such an experience? The church has just experienced a great victory and all some can do is complain.

C. Gideon minimized what he had done and maximized what others had done because he sought no praise (Judges 8:2).

V. When God Looks for a Partner He Looks for a Person Who Seeks No Power.

A. Thrilled with the victory they tried to make Gideon king (Judges 8:22).

B. Gideon refused.

C. The lust for power is pervasive in the world. Often it threatens the peace and harmony as well as the progress of the church.

VI. When God Looks for a Partner He Looks for a Person Who Seeks No Personal Gain.

A. It was the custom of soldiers in that day to plunder the fallen soldiers of the enemy.

B. The Midianite soldiers all wore golden ear rings.

C. Gideon said, "bring them all to me."

D. They did: 1700 shekels of gold!

E. Gideon made a beautiful decoration for the place of worship and kept for himself not one shekel. He was a man who sought no personal gain.

Conclusion

What happens when God finds such a partner? Israel enjoyed 40 years of peace!

Bringing in the Sheaves
Psalm 126:6

Introduction

Many know the old song: "Bringing in the Sheaves". Few know that it comes from an older song, from this text in the Psalms. Many will never have seen sheaves of wheat, but the image of those bundles of harvested grain still help us understand our task in world missions

I. Notice the Sorrow.

A. Why does the sower weep? He weeps because he knows that people are lost.
   1. Jesus believed that people were lost (Luke 19:10).
   2. The apostle Paul believed that people were lost (Romans 3:23; 6:27; 1 Timothy 2:4,5).
   3. The apostle Peter believed that people were lost (2 Peter 3:9).
   4. The apostle John believed that people were lost (John 3:16).
   5. I believe that people are lost.
   6. The church must believe that people are lost.
   7. If people are not lost Jesus died for nothing.

B. He weeps because many will reject the opportunity to be saved.
   1. Not all received Him (John 1:11,12).
   2. The parable of the sower shows this (Matthew 13:3 ff.).

II. Notice the Seed.

A. Why is it precious?
   1. Because there is no other like it.
   2. Because it cost so much. It cost the life of the Lord Jesus Christ.
   3. Because it can produce such a wonderful harvest.

B. Why is the good news called seed?
   1. It is like seed in that the soil (soul) must be prepared to receive it.
   2. It is like seed in that it takes time to germinate.
   3. It is like seed in that it takes the right conditions to germinate.

4. It is like seed in that it must be spread.

5. It is not like seed in one way. It never perishes (1 Peter 1:23).

III. Notice the Sower.

A. Some human being is necessary.

B. God could have used angels, but He chose instead to use us.

C. The sower must go somewhere (Matthew 28:19,20; Mark 16:15,16).

IV. Notice the Certain Harvest.

A. The *King James Version* uses the word doubtless.

B. It is easy for the sower to get discouraged.

C. We have, however, a promise of success (Isaiah 55:11).

Conclusion

Missions is not an option in the church of the Lord Jesus Christ. He has not given us that option. We must go. He told us to take the gospel. They need the gospel. They want the gospel. Only by the gospel can they be saved.

Illustrations

For years people who excavated the tombs of Egypt were disappointed. Grave robbers had been there before them. At last, however, they found the tomb of King Tutankahmen, commonly called King Tut. They were overjoyed. Robbers had not found it before them. Among the rich treasures of gold and precious stones, they found some seeds. They planted them. The seeds germinated and grew. They had been in that tomb for centuries, but they germinated and grew. It is no wonder that the gospel is compared to a seed.

The famous author Ring Lardner once said, "How can a man write if he can't cry?" We ask, "How can anyone believe the Bible and not cry?" Millions live their whole lives without any help from the Lord Jesus and die without any hope. It must break the heart of the church as it breaks the heart of God.

Three Models for New Leaders
Acts 13:1-3

Introduction
In both Old Testament and New we find some models for the passing of leadership from one to another. By putting all three together we can see three different aspects of the deed we do today.

I. The Scepter was Passed From Saul to David.

A.   2 Samuel 2:4 and 5:3-5.

B.   This shows us the transfer of responsibility.
1.   We choose the word responsibility rather than authority.
2.   We choose the word responsibility rather than power.

C.   King Saul was jealous of David, but there should be no jealousy among leaders.

D.   David showed that he deserved to lead when he did not seek revenge nor try to get even.

E.   David's double coronation was a unifying act. So good leaders should always work to unify never to divide.

F.   When David thought about a model for God's leadership, he thought of the shepherd, not of the King (Psalm 23:1). In every age good spiritual leaders must see themselves as shepherds.

II. The Robe was Passed From Elijah to Elisha.

A.   2 Kings 2:7-14.

B.   This shows us the transfer of ministry.
1.   Elisha did not ask to be greater than Elijah.
2.   He did ask to be allowed to continue Elijah's work.

C.   Then, as today, there were big shoes to be filled.

D.   "We are dwarfs standing on the shoulders of giants." We can see farther than they could, but only because of them.

E.   The robe was a prophet's robe.

F.   The robe was a servant's robe.

G.   It had nothing to do with fame, or influence, or personal power.

III. The Spirit Passed From Jesus To His Followers.

A.   Jesus was filled with the Spirit.
1.   This had been predicted (Luke 3.22).
2.   The prediction was fulfilled (Luke 4:18).

B.   Jesus in turn promised the Spirit to His disciples.
1.   John 14:26.
2.   John 16:13.
3.   John 20:22.

C.   That promise was kept.
1.   Acts 1:5.
2.   Acts 1:8.
3.   Acts 2:4.

D.   The Spirit meant power.
1.   It did not mean political power.
2.   It did not mean economic power.
3.   It did mean spiritual power.
4.   It is this power that we should seek, and only this power.

Conclusion

Those we set apart today will serve well if they accept responsibility, are willing to serve, and are open to God's power in their lives.

Footprints in the Sand
Joshua 14:6-13

Introduction

> *Lives of great men all remind us*
> *We can make our lives sublime;*
> *And departing leave behind us*
> *Footprints in the sands of time.*
> —Longfellow

I. He Was a Man of Undying Courage.

A. He had this courage when he was young.
1. Forty-five years before Caleb had been among the twelve spies.
2. It was not easy to go against the majority.
3. The names of the ten pessimistic spies are unknown!

B. His courage was undiminished by the passing of the years.
1. It is easy to be courageous for one decisive moment. It is more difficult to maintain that courage for a lifetime.
2. It is common to be courageous when you are young. Young people think they are indestructible. It is not so common when you are mature and know that you are mortal.

C. His courage was undiminished by the difficulties.
1. He chose the mountain when he might have chosen the well-watered plain of Jericho, the gentle hills of Galilee, the fertile fields of Esdraelon.
2. He chose the place where the soil was thin and farming was difficult.
3. He chose the place where the enemy was most deeply entrenched, and where it would be difficult to drive them out.
4. He didn't choose the mountain for the view! He chose it because it was difficult.

II. He Was a Man of Unflagging Faith.

A. He chose the difficult.
1. Some choose to serve the Lord in the place that will yield

61

the most results. Others choose the place that is the most difficult, the most remote, or the most dangerous.

2. We need both! Those who work in the productive field provide the resources for those who work in the resistant field. Those who work in the resistant field provide the inspiration for us all.

B. Caleb was an example to Israel. They could have occupied the land 40 years before! He is also an example to us!

III. He had an Unfailing Faith.

A. There is a religious reason for his choice. In Hebron was the burial place of Abraham, Sarah, and Isaac. It would be like an American choosing Arlington National Cemetery.

B. He had faith in himself. He believed that he could subdue the enemy, occupy the land, and make a living there.

C. He had faith in the future.
1. He was 85 years old when he made this choice. We can imagine a man making such a choice at 25, but at 85 he still had faith in the future.
2. So many people his age look with favor on the past, with fear on the present, and without faith to the future.

D. He had faith in God.

Conclusion

What an example Caleb is for people of any age.

Illustrations

"We can forgive a child that is afraid of the dark. We cannot forgive men who are afraid of the light." — Plato

When Anwar Sadat was assassinated, they buried him temporarily beside Egypt's Unknown Soldier. Their unknown soldier and their best known soldier lay side by side. So Joshua and Caleb stand side by side in Scripture: one well known, the other hardly known at all. You often meet someone named Joshua, seldom someone named Caleb.

New Clothes

Colossians 3:12-14

Introduction

Young people all over the world are keenly conscious of what they wear. They want to wear the latest styles. For that matter, so do older people. We don't want to wear clothes that suggest we are not up to date. The apostle Paul wrote these verses about new clothes.

I. Our New Clothes.

A. We have to have new clothes because when we were converted we became new creatures.
1. 2 Corinthians 5:17.
2. The old clothes don't suit the new creature.
3. Have you ever seen a dog wearing a sweater? When you did you knew that one creature was wearing something really intended for a different creature.

B. The new clothes suit us.
1. Compassion fits us perfectly
2. Kindness fits us, too.
3. Humility fits as if it were designed just for us.

C. The new clothes are becoming.
1. We're told that some people cannot wear some colors. The colors must go with your hair, your complexion, your eyes.
2. You look good in gentleness.
3. Patience is very becoming to you.
4. Since we have been forgiven, forgiveness to others suits us well.
5. The new clothes are held together by the belt of love.

D. We must wear them every day, not just on Sundays or special occasions.
1. They will never get soiled.
2. They will never wear out.
3. We will never outgrow them.
4. They will never go out of style.
5. They are not really new. Christ wore them before we did.

II. Our Old Clothes.

A. Before we can wear our new clothes we have to get rid of our old clothes. I have only given you half of my text. The other half is in Colossians 3:5-10.

B. We have to get rid of them because they don't fit any more.

C. We have to get rid of them because they aren't comfortable anymore.

D. They don't fit us because they didn't fit Christ. Can you imagine Christ doing any of these things?

E. They didn't fit Him because they were unsuitable for the climate of Heaven, from which He came and to which He went.

Conclusion

We all must decide to give up our old clothes and wear our new clothes. it is a decision we make in two ways. We make it decisively when we become Christians. We also must make it daily as we decide what spiritual clothes we will wear each day.

Illustration

In many major airports you can have fun watching the people. You can tell which ones have arrived from Florida or the Caribbean. They are wearing shorts and straw hats. You can tell which ones are arriving from the far north. They are wearing coats and overshoes and gloves. You can tell by their clothes where they have been. With Christians it is different. You can tell by our clothes where we are going.

At an atheist's funeral someone remarked that he was all dressed up with no place to go. We are all dressed up, and we have some place to go.